A PLACE FOR HARVEST

THE STORY *of* KENNY HIGASHI

Lauren R. Harris   ILLUSTRATED BY Felicia Hoshino

SOUTH DAKOTA HISTORICAL SOCIETY PRESS / PIERRE

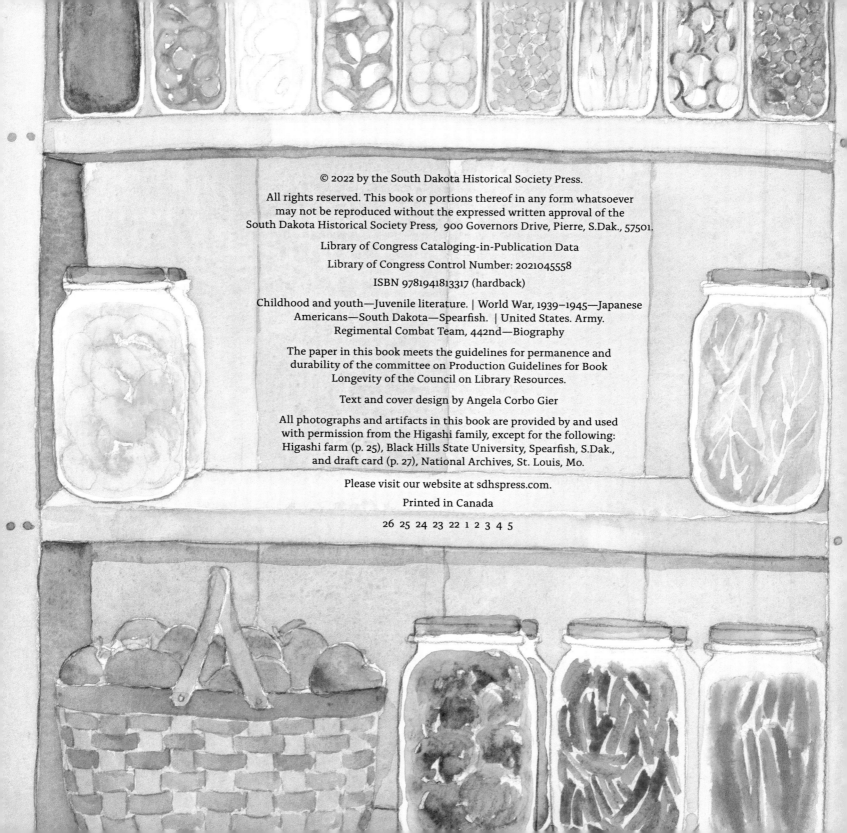

Library of Congress Cataloging-in-Publication Data

Library of Congress Control Number: 2021045558

ISBN 9781941813317 (hardback)

Childhood and youth—Juvenile literature. | World War, 1939–1945—Japanese Americans—South Dakota—Spearfish. | United States. Army. Regimental Combat Team, 442nd—Biography

The paper in this book meets the guidelines for permanence and durability of the committee on Production Guidelines for Book Longevity of the Council on Library Resources.

Text and cover design by Angela Corbo Gier

All photographs and artifacts in this book are provided by and used with permission from the Higashi family, except for the following: Higashi farm (p. 25), Black Hills State University, Spearfish, S.Dak., and draft card (p. 27), National Archives, St. Louis, Mo.

Please visit our website at sdhspress.com.

Printed in Canada

26 25 24 23 22 1 2 3 4 5

To Sherri, for writing stories with me long ago below the stage
— L. R. H.

To Sora and Yume, I learn so much from you every day
—F. H.

Kenny Higashi loved his hometown. He smiled and offered a helping hand to everyone he met.

Long ago, Kenny's dad journeyed from Japan to western South Dakota. Mr. Higashi was a farmer. He looked at the gold leaves of the aspens and smelled the spicy pines on the hills and in the canyons. He saw the wide prairies filled with waving grasses dotted with wildflowers.

He decided it was the perfect place for a harvest of happiness.

Mr. Higashi returned to Japan. He married his childhood sweetheart and brought her back to South Dakota. Kenny, his older brother Clarence, and their three little sisters were all born near the small town of Spearfish.

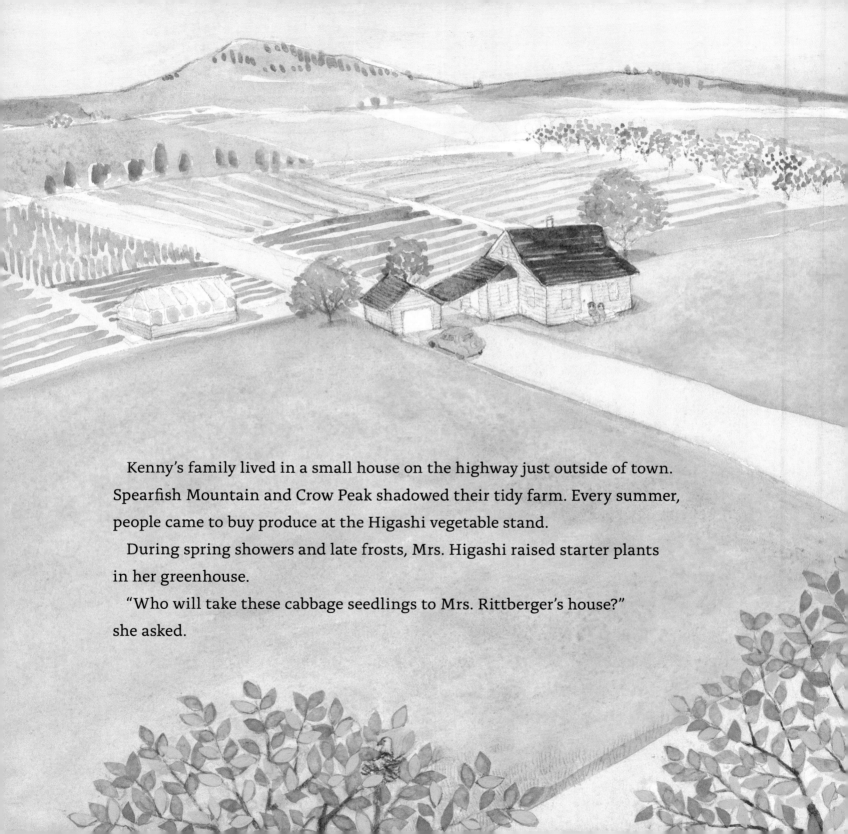

Kenny's family lived in a small house on the highway just outside of town. Spearfish Mountain and Crow Peak shadowed their tidy farm. Every summer, people came to buy produce at the Higashi vegetable stand.

During spring showers and late frosts, Mrs. Higashi raised starter plants in her greenhouse.

"Who will take these cabbage seedlings to Mrs. Rittberger's house?" she asked.

"I will!" Kenny said, with a smile. He loved to look for eagle's nests among the papery leaves of the cottonwood trees along the road.

3

During the summer, the family picked fruit from the trees they had planted on the farm. They watered and weeded rows and rows of tiny vegetables.

Later, they went down the rows, picking fat peas and bright orange carrots. They harvested plump ears of corn, bushy cabbages, and juicy tomatoes.

"I need someone to deliver this box of peaches to Mrs. Bern," said Mr. Higashi.

"I'll take it!" Kenny said, with a grin. He loved to ride his bike on the shaded path by Spearfish Creek, a shiny blue ribbon that bubbled merrily along the edge of town.

During the fall, Mr. Higashi sold drum-sized pumpkins and bags of crispy apples. Mrs. Higashi preserved produce for the winter in sparkling jars.

"Who wants to go fishing?" Mr. Higashi said when the work was done.

"I do!" Kenny smiled. He hoped to catch more fish than his dad.

Mr. Higashi put a worm on his hook and cast it into the water. The pole wiggled, and a fat trout flipped onto the bank. When their creels were full, Kenny had out-fished his dad by one.

"Well done, Kenny," said Mr. Higashi. "Hard work can bring a harvest of happiness, no matter what we're doing."

During short winter days and long winter nights, the family listened as tunes from the radio danced with the wind whistling down the chimney. Mrs. Higashi wrote letters to relatives in Japan. The little girls read books, and Kenny and his dad whittled fishing poles and toys. Clarence worked in the garage tuning up the car.

"I want to fix potatoes for supper, but we just ran out," Kenny's mom said one day. "Mr. Lown has plenty at his store in town, unless we would rather eat parsnips."

"I'll go get some!" Kenny said, with a smile. He loved the tall jars of colorful candies and the woody, sweet smells of Lown's Mercantile. Besides, he didn't care much for parsnips. Kenny pulled on his boots and coverall. Pretending to be a snowplow, he pushed his way through the deep drifts.

Sadness came to the Higashi family while Kenny was in high school. "WELL KNOWN SPEARFISH FARMER DIES," the newspaper headline said. Mrs. Higashi cried and worried about the future. Kenny was only eighteen years old, but he and Clarence took charge of the farm. Clarence fixed the tractor engine and tilled the soil. Kenny weeded long rows of vegetables. In the fall, their neighbors came and bought corn, carrots, and cabbages as usual.

The December after Kenny graduated from high school, Imperial Japan sent planes to bomb United States ships in Hawaii. Mrs. Higashi cried again. By New Year's Day, most of Kenny's school friends had become soldiers. Clarence and Kenny received letters from the United States government saying they could stay home because they were farmers. Lots of vegetables would be needed to feed South Dakota families.

One cold February morning, Kenny walked to his winter job at Lown's Mercantile. As he passed Mrs. Rittberger's house, she rushed out. "Oh, Kenny, I've read the news. We won't let anything happen to your family! You tell your mom I'll get my cabbage seedlings in the spring, just like always." She hurried back inside.

As he passed Mrs. Bern's house, she opened her door looking worried and gave him a jar full of peaches.

"I saw the morning paper," she said. "But don't worry, Kenny. No one will take your family away. You can count on it!"

Kenny walked into Lown's Mercantile. People were talking all at once.
Mr. Lown handed Kenny the newspaper. President Roosevelt was sending
all Japanese Americans to live together in camps far from their homes and
towns, the paper said. Armed guards would patrol these camps.

"The government is concerned that some Japanese Americans might be loyal to Japan instead of the United States," Kenny read.

"But my brother and sisters and I don't even speak or read Japanese," he said.

"Your family belongs here," Mr. Lown said. "We are all South Dakotans and Americans." Everyone cheered.

"The Higashi family is too important to this town," Mr. Lown continued. "We've made up our minds. Nobody's taking your family anywhere."

"If the government tells us we have to move, then we'll have no choice," Kenny said.

"We'll see about that," Mr. Lown said firmly.

All day, Kenny wondered what would happen to his family. He hurried home after work. Clarence was already back from his job at Junek's Auto Garage. Two men in military uniforms were there, too.

"We're supposed to tell you that your family will have to move to a guarded camp," one of the men said. "But we'll make a deal with you. One brother may stay here with the rest of your family and manage the farm. The other brother must join the army and protect our country."

"I'll go," Kenny said. "Clarence's mechanic and farming skills will help our family more right now." The next morning, Kenny left Spearfish.

Kenny trained hard alongside his new friends in the army. They served in an all-Japanese American division—the 100th Infantry Battalion. Most of the new soldiers were from Hawaii, California, or Washington.

"What's it like living all the way out in South Dakota?" one man asked.

"It's the only place I've ever known," Kenny said. "We're happy there. Hard work can bring a good harvest no matter where you are," he added.

The young soldiers sailed together across the sea to the war in Europe. When his new friends wondered where to find food while marching, Kenny smiled and said, "I'll help." From an icy stream he caught fat fish with his bare hands.

When the enemy trapped another battalion of the United States Army deep in a forest in France, Kenny and his unit were there to help. They fought through snow drifts and freezing rain to rescue the men of the Lost Battalion.

Many of Kenny's friends were killed or hurt, but when troops were needed in Italy, his unit pressed on. Just before the war ended, Kenny was wounded in both legs. Two men in uniforms came to the hospital to give him the Purple Heart, a medal for bravery and courage.

"Thank you for your hard work and loyalty, Sergeant Higashi," one said. "Would you like to go home now?"

"Yes, sir, I'll go!" Kenny said with a smile.

Back in South Dakota, the bus bumped and swerved along the snowy road.

"Almost home, Soldier," said the bus driver. "Glad you made it."

"Thanks," Kenny said. "Me too."

The bus lurched around a corner, and people waved and shouted greetings to Kenny. His heart began to thump happily.

"I bet you've seen a bunch of wonderful places," said the bus driver.

"Oh, sure!" Kenny said. "I climbed up the Leaning Tower of Pisa. I swam in the Mediterranean Sea, and I walked through cathedrals in Rome."

"Wow!" the bus driver exclaimed. "Which place was your favorite?"

"This one!" Kenny pointed at the busy shops of downtown Spearfish. "Home is the happiest place for me."

KENNY'S WORLD

Kenny, ca. 1922

Kiwano and Shiichi Higashi, Kenny's dad and mom, ca. 1918

Clarence holding his sister, ca. 1925

Kenneth Ray Higashi was born on December 23, 1921, in Belle Fourche, South Dakota, just north of Spearfish. He was the second of five siblings: Clarence, Kenny, Mae, Jean, and Lily. The family moved into Spearfish when Kenny was seven. They managed a vegetable farm in the same location for fifty years.

Kenny and his friend Buster Wopat

In February 1942, President Franklin D. Roosevelt signed Executive Order 9066. It forced more than one hundred thousand Japanese Americans out of their homes and into guarded compounds. When the two government men came to visit Clarence and Kenny in Spearfish, they took away the family's shotgun and radio and told them that they might be moved to one of the guarded camps. People in Spearfish recall that the townspeople planned to refuse the government's order and protect the Higashi family.

Kenny joined the 100th Infantry Battalion, C Company. All the enlisted men were Japanese Americans. The battalion fought as part of the 442nd Regimental Combat Team. Kenny became a sergeant and earned sixteen medals for bravery and service, including the Purple Heart. The 100th/442nd traveled across North Africa and Europe, going wherever the United States Army needed them.

Kenny especially recalled the battle to rescue the Lost Battalion of 275 American soldiers who became separated when the German army surrounded them. The 100th/442nd fought for four days and nights in freezing weather to save the trapped soldiers. Kenny and his buddy took turns sleeping in a foxhole for one hour, then fighting for one hour, until the Lost Battalion was finally free.

After the war, Kenny returned to Spearfish, where he worked for the United States Postal Service for thirty years. He got married, enjoyed golf and bowling, and in November 2020, he died just a short ways from the little white house where he grew up.

Sugar beet crop, Higashi farm, 1930s

"GO FOR BROKE"
The 100th Infantry Battalion and 442nd Regimental Combat Team

The nation of Japan bombed Pearl Harbor in Hawaii on December 7, 1941. Thousands of Nisei— young Americans whose parents were Japanese immigrants—lived in Hawaii and wanted to join the United States Armed Services. They were angry about Imperial Japan's attack and eager to prove their loyalty to the United States. The government finally allowed them to enlist in an all-Japanese American unit called the 100th Infantry Battalion. The army also drafted fifteen hundred Nisei from the United States mainland to serve in World War II. Many of these young men had endured harassment and suspicion in their home communities. Almost all had left their families behind barbed-wire fences in incarceration camps across the United States.

Army leaders were unsure about sending the all-Japanese American group into battle, so some recruits served in the Military Intelligence Service, where they interpreted Japanese military messages from the war in the Pacific Ocean. The remainder trained for fourteen months in Wisconsin and Mississippi. Hawaiian-born Nisei brought some local customs and sayings with them, which the other soldiers adopted. The unit's motto became "Go for Broke," which means to gamble everything in a card game in order to win. The 100th threw themselves into their training. The only trouble the army had with them was finding uniforms that fit properly. Most of the young men were shorter and smaller than the average American soldier.

In 1943, the 100th shipped overseas to help fight against the German army. They and more Nisei recruits made up the 442nd Regimental Combat Team. The 100th/442nd earned a reputation for strength, endurance, and persistence as they fought through North Africa, Italy, France, and Germany. When one soldier could not fight anymore, another stepped in and took his place. This continual flood of willing Japanese American soldiers meant that the 100th/442nd suffered many casualties. Today, it is known as the Purple

Heart Battalion because over nine thousand of its soldiers earned the medal for injury or death during combat. The 100th/442nd is the most highly decorated unit of its size in United States history.

The 100th/442nd won many seemingly impossible victories. Grateful villagers gave them food and did their laundry. Soldiers in other units respected their skill and intense determination to win, calling them "Little Iron Men." General Mark W. Clark, their commanding officer, once said, "I have absolute faith in every soldier in the 100th."

After the war, President Harry Truman held a special ceremony for the 100th/442nd. They were the only unit that President Truman welcomed back from the war in person. "You are to be congratulated on what you have done for this great country of ours," he told them. "You fought not only the enemy, but you fought prejudice—and you have won."

Since 1999, the Go For Broke Monument in Los Angeles, California, celebrates the patriotism of these veterans. A sloping, black-granite stone records the names of over sixteen thousand Japanese Americans who served during World War II.

Kenny in uniform, ca. 1945

SOURCES: General Clark, quoted in Col. Young Oak Kim, *Puka Puka Parade* (May-June 1981): 5–6; President Truman, "Remarks upon Presenting a Citation to a Nisei Regiment, July 15, 1946," Public Papers of Harry S Truman, National Archives, Washington, D.C.; "442nd Regimental Combat Team," www.the442org; Go For Broke National Education Center, www.goforbroke.org.

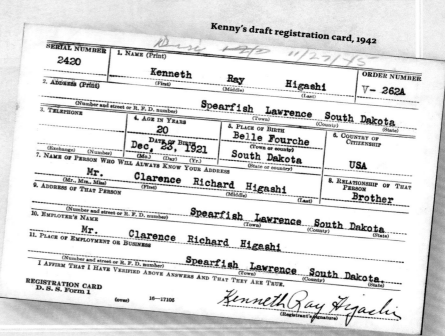

Kenny's draft registration card, 1942

AUTHOR'S NOTE

I first learned about the 100th Infantry Battalion and 442nd Regimental Combat Team while researching a family story about the 1944 Lost Battalion rescue. I mentioned the all-Japanese American regiment to friends, who told me that Kenny Higashi lived just a few miles from me. After meeting him, I wrote a front-page newspaper article about him for Veteran's Day. Many people who had known Kenny all his life contacted me, saying they never knew the details of his heroic wartime service.

As I interviewed him for that story and later, Kenny gave me a special treasure—one of the arm patches from his original World War II service uniform. It is the official Go For Broke insignia: Lady Liberty's arm holding up the torch inside the shape of a coffin.

I would like to thank the Go For Broke National Education Center for its commitment to preserve the legacy of the 100th/442nd. I also thank Jeff Morita, member of Sons and Daughters of the 442nd Regimental Combat Team in Hawaii, for his extra research and for nominating Kenny for the French Legion of Honor medal. I am especially grateful to Dale and Marylee Bell for introducing me to Kenny and encouraging me to write about him.

FURTHER READING

Hanal, Rachel. *The Japanese American Internment: An Interactive History Adventure.* Mankato, Minn.: Capstone Press, 2008.

Harris, Lauren R. *The Plum Neighbor.* Los Angeles: Go For Broke National Educational Center Books, 2019.

Malaspina, Ann. *A Scarf for Keiko.* Minneapolis: Kar-Ben Publishing, 2019.

Mochizuki, Ken. *Heroes.* Illus, Dom Lee. New York: Lee & Low Books, 1995.

Grady, Cynthia. *Write to Me: Letters from Japanese American Children to the Librarian They Left Behind.* Watertown, Mass.: Charlesbridge, 2018.

Yabu, Shigero. *Hello, Maggie!* Camarillo, Calif.: Yabitoon Books, 2007.